Recipes for
Kindness
Book 1

What we love most about Christmas
are the stories about ordinary folks
doing extraordinary things.

Whether it's people surprising less-fortunate families
with gifts under the tree or neighbors taking a few moments
to sweep your walk after a snowstorm, these small
kindnesses carry us throughout the year.

Everyone aspires to that spirit of giving but sometimes,
it can get lost in the holiday hustle & bustle.

In this little book, we've gathered a sampling of stories from our **Gooseberry Patch** family to touch your heart, plus our favorite ideas for reaching out at this special time of year.

You'll also find best-loved recipes to make & give and favorites to treat your own family too...there are even a few crafts to try and all the inspiration we could fit.

We hope this season finds you slowing down to appreciate the thoughtfulness of others and cooking up your own recipes for kindness!

Visits with my 98-year-old mother are spent recalling good times, talking about her favorite memories and usually, enjoying a treat from home. These visits to her nursing home also give me the opportunity to meet her many friends there. Quite social even at advanced ages, their stories never fail to warm my heart.

Whether it's their memories of baking cookies at Christmas, stitching little clothes for grandchildren or recalling a favorite hobby, their richly detailed stories of days gone by are such a pleasure.

Taking the time to learn everyone's name, asking about visits from family members or just sitting down to chat about the weather is often as beneficial for me as it is for them.

As much as this little book is all about reaching out to give back in tangible ways, sometimes kindness isn't about concrete things. Something as simple as giving your time and attention can make the biggest difference of all.

~ Vickie

No act of
kindness,
however small,
is ever wasted.

~ *Aesop*

Tips for Holiday Kindness

For neighbors, friends & family

Attending a holiday gathering? Take a few candid photos and share with the hostess when you send along a thank-you note.

Christmas cards are mailed by the dozen but when it comes to special family members, include a personal note letting them know how much their love and support means to you.

The holidays are full of activity for adults and kids alike. If you're taking your child to choir practice or a school event, volunteer to pick up other nearby kids too and give their parents an unexpected break.

For your community

Organize a clothing or food drive with co-workers, your book club or a church group. Nonperishable items and cold-weather wear are always welcome at family shelters...tasty treats, litter and leashes will be appreciated at animal shelters too!

When giving tokens of appreciation to teachers, take a moment to write a personal note as well. Don't forget the school nurse, secretary and bus driver...they're all entrusted with an important job!

Spending a day doing all your holiday baking? Fix up a special plate for your local police or fire department...a great way to say thanks for keeping us safe year 'round.

Make holiday shopping a little less stressful when you offer to return a shopping cart to the store for someone loading a car. Helping a senior to load in the groceries will be appreciated too!

For folks you've never met

Extra coupons for baking staples and holiday favorites will be fun to find on grocery shelves...and it doesn't cost you a dime!

Random acts of kindness are as fun for the giver as they are the recipient. Drop an extra coin or two into vending machines or car washes when there are people waiting and enjoy the feeling all day long.

Kindness begins at home so why not treat your family to these best-loved recipes this holiday season...they're sure to feel how special they are!

Breakfast Pizza

Easy to whip up and so fun to eat!

8-oz. tube refrigerated crescent
    rolls
1 lb. ground sausage, browned
    and drained
1 c. frozen diced potatoes, thawed
1 c. shredded Cheddar cheese

5 eggs
1/4 c. milk
1/2 t. salt
1/8 t. pepper
2 T. grated Parmesan cheese

Separate rolls into 8 triangles. Arrange rolls with points toward the center in an ungreased 12" pizza pan. Press over bottom and up sides to form crust; seal perforations. Spoon browned sausage over crust. Sprinkle with potatoes; top with Cheddar cheese. Set aside. Beat together eggs, milk, salt and pepper. Pour over crust. Sprinkle Parmesan cheese over top. Bake at 375 degrees for 25 to 30 minutes. Cut into wedges to serve. Makes 6 servings.

*Put a Mexican spin on this pizza and have a breakfast fiesta!
Add a few spoonfuls of chopped green chiles to the eggs
and use Pepper Jack cheese instead of Cheddar!*

Ready-in-an-Hour Bread

Tastes like it took all day…only you'll know how easy it really is!

3 to 4 c. all-purpose flour, divided
1 env. active dry yeast
1 T. sugar
1 t. salt
1/2 c. water
1/3 c. milk
1 T. butter
2 eggs, divided

Combine 1-1/2 cups flour, yeast, sugar and salt in a large bowl; set aside. Heat water, milk and butter over medium heat, stirring occasionally, for 5 minutes, or until butter is melted. Do not boil. Remove from heat and stir into flour mixture. Add one egg, stirring to combine. Add enough of remaining flour to make dough easy to handle but not too stiff. On lightly floured surface, knead dough about 5 minutes, or until smooth and springy. Form into a loaf. Place on a lightly greased baking sheet or baking stone; cover and let rise in a warm place for 30 minutes. Beat remaining egg and brush over entire loaf with a pastry brush. Bake at 400 degrees for 15 to 20 minutes, or until golden. Makes one loaf.

Giving a loaf of homebaked goodness this holiday? Make this bread extra special with a sprinkle of fresh herbs, Parmesan cheese or poppy seed…just sprinkle after brushing with egg and bake as usual.

Mom's Bacon-Cheddar Meatloaf

The savory aroma that fills the house while this is baking lets everyone know that dinner will be extra tasty tonight!

1 lb. bacon, crisply cooked,
    crumbled and divided
1-1/2 lbs. ground beef sirloin
1-1/2 c. shredded Cheddar cheese
2 eggs, beaten
1/3 c. bread crumbs
1/3 c. mayonnaise

1 T. Worcestershire sauce
1/2 t. salt
1/2 t. pepper
1/2 c. catsup
1/4 t. hot pepper sauce
3 T. Dijon mustard

Set aside 1/2 cup bacon for topping. Combine remaining bacon with next 8 ingredients in a large bowl; set aside. Mix remaining ingredients in a small bowl; set aside 3 tablespoons of mixture for topping. Add remaining catsup mixture to sirloin mixture; blend well. Press into an ungreased 9"x5" loaf pan; spread reserved catsup mixture over top and sprinkle with reserved bacon. Bake, uncovered, at 350 degees for 50 to 60 minutes. Remove from oven and let stand 5 to 10 minutes before slicing. Serves 6 to 8.

Double this recipe and bake an extra for a busy mom you know! Just line the loaf pan with aluminum foil and, once baked and cooled, lift out of the pan. Wrap it up in a new piece of foil and it's ready to freeze!

Old-Fashioned Chicken & Dumplin's

Hot and hearty…just the thing to warm up winter!

2 boneless, skinless chicken
    breasts, cut into strips
1/8 t. salt
1/8 t. pepper
1 T. olive oil
2 T. all-purpose flour
14-1/2 oz. can chicken broth
1 c. water

1 onion, sliced
1 c. green beans
1 c. carrots, peeled and shredded
2/3 c. biscuit baking mix
1/3 c. cornmeal
1/4 c. shredded Cheddar cheese
1/2 c. milk

Sprinkle chicken with salt and pepper; brown with oil in a Dutch oven or stockpot. Sprinkle flour over the top; stir in broth, water, onion, beans and carrots. Bring to a boil; reduce heat and simmer for 5 minutes. In another bowl, combine baking mix, cornmeal and cheese; stir in milk. Drop by tablespoonfuls into soup; return to a boil. Simmer, covered, for 10 to 12 minutes. Serves 4.

This recipe is great for
using up leftover turkey
after the big feast too!

11

Rich Chocolate Crinkles

So fudgy...enjoy them with an icy cold glass of milk.

1/2 c. oil
4 1-oz. sqs. unsweetened baking
    chocolate, melted
2 c. sugar
4 eggs

2 t. vanilla extract
1/2 t. salt
2 c. all-purpose flour
2 t. baking powder
1 c. powdered sugar

Mix oil, chocolate and sugar. Add eggs one at a time, until well mixed. Add vanilla, salt, flour and baking powder. Chill for several hours to overnight. Shape dough into balls of about one teaspoon each and roll in powdered sugar. Place about 2 inches apart on a well-greased baking sheet. Bake at 350 degrees for 10 to 12 minutes. Makes about 4 dozen.

This recipe makes a bunch and they're great for sharing. Stack 3 or 4 cookies inside a cello bag and tie with a wide ribbon...so pretty left on a neighbor's doorstep!

Apple-Cinnamon Dumplings

What a way to welcome the kids home for Christmas break!

2-1/2 c. all-purpose flour
4 t. baking powder
1 t. salt
3/4 c. shortening
1/2 c. milk

6 to 8 apples, peeled and cored
2 c. sugar
2 c. water
1 t. cinnamon

Mix together flour, baking powder, salt, shortening and milk. Roll out pastry; cut into squares large enough to cover each apple. Place apples in center of squares and bring corners of pastry up and over; pinch to seal. Place dumplings in a greased 13"x9" baking pan. Combine sugar, water and cinnamon in a saucepan; heat to boiling and then cool slightly. Spoon one-third of the mixture over dumplings. Bake at 350 degrees for 45 to 60 minutes, spooning additional sauce over the dumplings twice during baking. Makes 6 to 8 servings.

Before baking, add a few raisins
and a little butter inside each
apple for an extra-special treat.

Like many college students, I was eagerly anticipating winter break and spending the holidays with family at home. After finals, I hopped into my little car and set out for the long drive home.

Long before the days of debit cards, I knew that I had enough cash in my pocket for gas (and a cup of coffee or two) on my way. At the halfway point, I stopped to fill my tank and take a break. When I stepped up to the counter to pay, I was surprised to find my pocket empty!

Maybe my cash had fallen out in the car, I thought, or maybe I'd stashed the bill in my purse instead. After a frantic search, I was still empty-handed. I'd already filled my tank and was still hours from home!

I went back inside and tried to explain, my voice becoming shakier by the moment. Just as I was asking to use the phone to call home, a stranger stepped forward and handed me a crisp $20 bill.

Overcome with relief, I thanked him again & again. When I asked for his address so I could repay him, he refused. "Consider it your Christmas present!" he said with a smile as he walked out.

I'll never forget that small kindness, arriving just when I needed it most.

~ Jamie at **Gooseberry Patch**

Thank You!

It may seem like such a simple thing, but
following up gifts, invitations and even dinners
with a heartfelt thank-you note is one of
the easiest ways to be kind.

Especially during the Christmas season,
when we can get overwhelmed with generosity,
taking just a few moments to drop a card in the mail
allows you time to slow down and really appreciate
the kindness of others.

Treat neighbors, co-workers or a church group to a delicious surprise! Each of these recipes is not only tasty but perfectly portable too...easy to make & give!

Cranberry-Almond Breakfast Cake

Homemade from the heart, it's so pretty too!

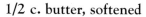

1/2 c. butter, softened	1 c. sour cream
1 c. sugar	1-1/2 t. almond extract, divided
2 eggs	16-oz. can whole-berry
2 c. all-purpose flour	cranberry sauce
1 t. baking soda	1/2 c. slivered almonds
1 t. baking powder	3/4 c. powdered sugar
1 t. salt	2 T. warm water

Blend butter and sugar together. Add eggs one at a time, beating well after each; set aside. Combine flour, baking soda, baking powder and salt; stir dry ingredients into butter mixture alternately with sour cream. Add one teaspoon extract. Pour half the batter into a greased and floured Bundt® pan. Spread cranberry sauce and almonds over batter. Top with remaining batter. Bake at 350 degrees for 50 to 55 minutes. Cool 5 minutes before removing from pan. Combine powdered sugar, water and remaining extract until smooth; spoon over cake before serving. Makes 12 servings.

Make a few copies of the recipe before toting this treat to potlucks or open houses...there are sure to be requests for it!

Razzleberry Swirl Muffins

Blueberries, blackberries or any berry…they're all delicious in this recipe!

2 c. all-purpose flour
1 c. brown sugar, packed
1-1/2 t. baking powder
1 t. baking soda
1/2 t. salt
1 c. quick-cooking oats,
   uncooked

2 eggs, beaten
1/3 c. oil
2 t. vanilla extract
1-1/2 c. buttermilk
3 to 4 c. frozen whole
   raspberries

Combine flour, brown sugar, baking powder, baking soda, salt and oats; set aside. Combine eggs, oil, vanilla and buttermilk in a separate bowl; blend well. Pour egg mixture over flour mixture and stir just until moistened; set aside. Place frozen berries in a large plastic zipping bag; seal and crush using a rolling pin. Measure out 2 cups crushed berries. Gently stir them into flour mixture and spoon batter into 12 paper-lined muffin cups. Bake at 375 degrees for 20 to 25 minutes. Makes one dozen.

Sending kids off to a Christmas break slumber party? Fix a batch of these muffins for everyone to enjoy at breakfast…a thoughtful way to thank their hostess in advance!

Chicken Salad Casserole

Slivered almonds add delicious crunch to this potluck favorite!

4 c. cooked chicken, diced
1/2 c. green onions, chopped
1 c. celery, chopped
2/3 c. slivered almonds
1/4 c. green olives with pimentos, sliced

10-3/4 oz. can cream of chicken soup
1 c. mayonnaise
1 t. lemon juice
2 c. shredded Cheddar cheese

Combine all ingredients except cheese; mix well. Spread into an ungreased 13"x9" baking pan; sprinkle cheese over top. Bake, uncovered, at 325 degrees for 25 minutes, or until cheese is melted and bubbly. Serves 10 to 12.

Pick up a few freshly baked croissants to go along with this warm and filling dish.

Can't-Stop-Munching Mix

Drop off some of this savory snack mix for a neighbor who's traveling this holiday!

1 c. mini pretzels	2 T. brown sugar, packed
1 c. corn chips	1 t. Worcestershire sauce
1 c. oyster crackers	1 t. chili powder
1 c. toasted pumpkin seeds	1/2 t. onion salt
1 c. honey-roasted peanuts	1/2 t. ground cumin
2 T. margarine, melted	1/8 t. cayenne pepper

Combine first 5 ingredients in a large bowl, tossing to mix. Whisk together remaining ingredients in a small bowl; pour over pretzel mixture and stir to coat. Spread into an ungreased roasting pan. Bake, covered, at 300 degrees for 25 minutes, stirring halfway through baking time. Cool completely; store in an airtight container.
Makes about 5 cups.

*Packaging this mix to go?
Use individual size containers...
the kids will love having
their very own.*

Tropical Dream Cake

Fluffy and full of fruit…it's like a slice of sunshine!

18-1/2 oz. pkg. yellow cake mix
1/4 c. applesauce
4 eggs, beaten
11-oz. can mandarin oranges
8-oz. container frozen whipped
    topping, thawed

3.4-oz. pkg. instant vanilla
    pudding mix
15-1/2 oz. can crushed
    pineapple, undrained

Combine cake mix, applesauce, eggs and oranges with their juice; mix well. Pour batter into a lightly greased 13"x9" baking pan. Bake at 350 degrees for 30 to 40 minutes, or until a toothpick inserted in the center removes clean; set aside to cool completely. Blend remaining ingredients together; spread over cooled cake. Refrigerate until ready to serve. Serves 16.

This cake is packed with vitamin C…doubly thoughtful for a friend feeling under the weather!

Chocolate-Mint Diamonds

Extra-fudgy brownies cut diagonally for a pretty presentation.

1 c. all-purpose flour
1 c. sugar
1 c. plus 6 T. butter, softened
    and divided
4 eggs, beaten
16-oz. can chocolate syrup

2 c. powdered sugar
1 T. water
1/2 t. mint extract
3 drops green food coloring
1 c. semi-sweet chocolate chips

Beat flour, sugar, 1/2 cup butter, eggs and syrup in a large bowl; pour into a greased 13"x9" baking pan. Bake at 350 degrees for 25 to 30 minutes, or until top springs back when lightly touched. Cool in pan. Combine powdered sugar and 1/2 cup butter, water, extract and food coloring in a medium bowl; beat until smooth. Spread over cooled brownie layer; chill until set. Melt chocolate chips and remaining butter in a double boiler, stirring until smooth. Pour over chilled mint layer; cover and chill again until firm. Cut diagonally into diamonds to serve. Makes 4 to 5 dozen.

Instead of mixing up the mint
filling, use raspberry preserves
   for a whole new taste!

With both of our families living close by, we thought the first few weeks home with our newborn daughter would be a breeze. Little did we know how much time one little baby can take!

In preparation, I'd made lasagna and a few other casseroles for the freezer but, looking back now, I must've thought 3 days was all it would take to get back to normal.

Sleep-deprived and getting pretty tired of sandwiches, we welcomed a neighbor couple for what we thought was just a social visit. Imagine our surprise when, along with a sweet gift for the baby, they carried in 3 huge shopping bags.

Katie went straight to the kitchen and started putting things away. Handing the baby off, I followed to help and to thank her.

Not content to just bring a token treat, they'd brought components for almost two weeks of easy meals, including a few of her homemade pizza crusts, sauce and toppings.

Their generosity was so appreciated and cemented our friendship. About a year later, when they welcomed their son, we were right there with Katie's famous pizza crust!

~Jen at **Gooseberry Patch**

Always be a little
kinder
than necessary.
~ *James M. Barrie*

Surprising a new mom this holiday? Perhaps you're taking a treat over to someone who can't get out often...regardless of the reason, these recipes are delicious, easy to make and will keep well in the freezer too!

Best-Ever Chili

Drop it off in a slow cooker or ladle into containers for easy-to-reheat single servings!

1 lb. ground beef
1/2 to 1 lb. bacon, chopped
1 onion, chopped
1/2 green pepper, diced
2 15-oz. cans dark red kidney
  beans, drained and rinsed
16-oz. can light red kidney beans,
  drained and rinsed
16-oz. can pinto beans, drained
  and rinsed

16-oz. can pork & beans
15-1/2 oz. can Sloppy Joe mix
14-1/2 oz. can diced tomatoes,
  drained and juice reserved
1/4 to 1/2 c. brown sugar,
  packed
salt, pepper and chili powder
  to taste

Brown ground beef and bacon with onion and green pepper; drain. Combine meat mixture with remaining ingredients in a slow cooker, using half of reserved tomato juice. Cover and cook on high setting until chili is heated through, about one hour; reduce heat to low setting and cook another 2 to 4 hours. Add remaining tomato juice if needed. Serves 6 to 8.

Homemade Pizza Crust

Freeze ahead of time and deliver with sauce, cheese and toppings…just a little assembly and dinner's done!

1 t. olive oil
1 t. sugar
1 c. warm water
    (110 to 115 degrees)
1 env. active dry yeast

Optional: salt, pepper, dried
    oregano, dried basil and
    garlic powder to taste
3-1/2 c. all-purpose flour,
    divided

Combine oil, sugar and water in a bowl. Add yeast, stirring to dissolve; set mixture aside. Add salt, pepper and spices to flour if desired. Add 3 cups flour, one cup at a time, to yeast mixture until dough is easy to handle. Knead on a floured surface until it is no longer sticky, adding remaining flour as needed. Flatten and shape as desired; cover and let rise 30 minutes before baking or freezing. Makes one crust.

To prepare, just spread with pizza sauce and add toppings and cheese of your choice. Bake at 400 degrees for 15 to 20 minutes until cheese is melted and crust is golden.

For easy freezing, flatten dough into crust, wrap in plastic wrap and then carefully fold into quarters.

Easy Cheesy Enchiladas

Enjoy it now or save for later…it's all up to the lucky recipient!

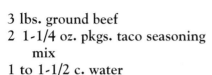

3 lbs. ground beef
2 1-1/4 oz. pkgs. taco seasoning
   mix
1 to 1-1/2 c. water
16-oz. can refried beans
2 pkgs. 10-inch flour tortillas
10-3/4 oz. can cream of
   mushroom soup

10-3/4 oz. can cream of
   chicken soup
2 10-oz. cans tomatoes
   with chiles
1-1/2 lbs. pasteurized process
   cheese spread, cubed

Brown ground beef in a Dutch oven over medium heat; drain. Add seasoning and water; simmer for 5 minutes. Add beans; cook for an additional 5 minutes. Spread mixture down center of tortillas; roll up. Arrange seam-side down in two lightly greased 13"x9" baking pans; set aside. Combine remaining ingredients in a medium saucepan; cook over medium heat until cheese is melted. Spoon over enchiladas. If freezing, cool and then cover tightly with aluminum foil. If serving immediately, bake, covered, at 350 degrees for 15 minutes, until bubbly. Makes 2 pans of 6 to 8 servings each.

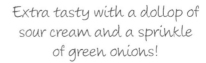

Extra tasty with a dollop of sour cream and a sprinkle of green onions!

Freezer-Friendly Layered Ravioli

All the flavors of lasagna in a fraction of the time!

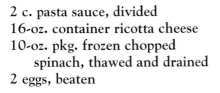

2 c. pasta sauce, divided
16-oz. container ricotta cheese
10-oz. pkg. frozen chopped
    spinach, thawed and drained
2 eggs, beaten

salt and pepper to taste
1/2 c. grated Romano or
    Parmesan cheese
18-oz. bag frozen cheese ravioli
1/2 c. shredded mozzarella cheese

Spread 1/2 cup pasta sauce in an ungreased, deep 8"x8" baking pan.
In a bowl, blend ricotta, spinach, eggs, salt, pepper and Romano or
Parmesan cheese. Layer one-third of the ravioli in the baking pan; top
with half the ricotta mixture. Repeat layering, ending with remaining
ravioli. Spoon remaining pasta sauce over top; sprinkle with mozzarella
cheese. Cover with aluminum foil and bake at 375 degrees for 40 minutes.
Remove foil and continue baking an additional 10 minutes. Serves 4 to 6.

*Don't forget the bread...pick up a loaf on your way to drop this
dish off or whip up our easy one-hour recipe on page 9!*

Peanut Butter Crunch Cookies

These will delight kids (and moms!) of all ages.

3/4 c. crunchy peanut butter	1 egg
1/2 c. shortening	1-3/4 c. all-purpose flour
1-1/4 c. brown sugar, packed	3/4 t. salt
3 T. milk	3/4 t. baking soda
1 T. vanilla extract	Optional: sugar for sprinkling

Combine peanut butter, shortening, brown sugar, milk and vanilla. Beat with an electric mixer on medium speed until well-blended. Add egg and beat just until blended. Combine dry ingredients. Add to peanut butter mixture at low speed. Drop by heaping teaspoonfuls onto an ungreased baking sheet. Flatten slightly in criss-cross pattern with tines of a fork. Sprinkle with sugar, if desired. Bake at 375 degrees for 7 to 8 minutes, or until set and golden. Makes 3 dozen.

Paper CD sleeves make great packages for oversized cookies!
Decorate with stamps and a fun tag...get creative but the real
hero is the yummy cookie peeking out the window.

Last-Minute Banana Bread

Takes just one bowl and a few minutes to whip up this favorite…it's so easy!

1/3 c. oil	2-1/3 c. biscuit baking mix
3 bananas, mashed	1 c. sugar
1/2 t. vanilla extract	1/2 c. chopped walnuts
3 eggs	

Beat together all ingredients for about 30 seconds. Pour batter into a greased 9"x5" loaf pan. Bake at 350 degrees for 35 to 45 minutes, or until a toothpick inserted in center comes out clean. Makes one loaf.

Individually wrapped mini loaves will be welcome surprises when left on co-workers' desks or dropped off in the teachers' lounge…keep one at home to enjoy with your morning coffee!

When you can't be with loved ones at the holidays, sending a personalized care package can be the next best thing. It's a thoughtful way to let them know you're thinking of them at Christmastime and all year 'round!

For parents & grandparents

They're sure to miss you even more at this time of year so gather up some goodies to send their way. Tuck in treats baked from a favorite family recipe along with a note to let them know how special they are. Add a movie you know they'll enjoy (or one you've enjoyed together!) and some yummy popcorn. A new date book or calendar with everyone's birthdays already noted is sure to be appreciated and, of course, updated photos of you and your family are always welcome...a note or drawing from the kids will be treasured forever!

Send them on their way with love when you gather up items to make their traveling time more fun! Include a batch of home-made goodies and a thermos of coffee or hot cocoa to warm

For anyone hitting the road for holiday travel

them up. Add some magazines or crossword puzzles for Mom & Dad plus a few travel-friendly toys to keep little ones occupied on the drive to Grandma's house. Toss in a gift card to a quick-stop restaurant along the way and they'll really appreciate your thoughtfulness.

For a far-away friend

Let your memories together be your guide when selecting small gifts you know she'll enjoy. A sweet indulgence baked from a decadent recipe, a CD from the band you saw together, a childhood picture of the two of you and a bottle of luxurious lotion in her favorite scent will make her feel loved. Stationery, a fun pen and a book of stamps will help you keep in touch...add a gift card for her local coffee shop, bookstore or a favorite boutique so she can treat herself when the busy holidays are over.

For holiday house guests

Welcome kids home from college, relatives in from out of town or friends visiting for the season with some extra-special touches. They'll love fluffy towels and yummy-smelling soaps in the bath and a delicious tea or cocoa mix tucked into a new mug on the nightstand. Leave a neighborhood map and a guide to favorite locations if they're new in town, and if they're bringing kids along, put together a mini care package for them too...crayons, fun stickers, books or special toys will make everyone feel welcome.

Get creative with your packaging this holiday and the outside will be almost as special as the inside! Try out these alternatives to traditional wrapping paper and gift bags... think of them as the icing on the cake!

Wrap It Up!
Clever twists on wrapping paper

⭐ Zoom in on text or pictures in the newspaper using a copier

⭐ Butcher paper decorated with handprints or drawings

⭐ Vintage tea towels, napkins or other linens

⭐ Last Sunday's comics or copies of vintage maps

Tie It On!
Clever ribbon replacements

⭐ Long strips of paper with fun punched-out shapes

⭐ Rick rack in bright colors and varying widths

⭐ Fluffy tinsel...add an ornament for extra sparkle

⭐ Jeweled ponytail holders gather tissue paper in style

⭐ Jute, twine or kitchen string

Cherry on Top!

Little add-ons and finishing touches

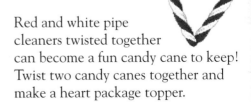

Make a tag out of
a photocopied vintage photo, holiday
card or vintage Christmas seal.

Cut a tiny mitten
out of felt and attach to a
clothespin with glue. Clip it onto
ribbon for an extra sweet touch.

Stitch up a homespun yo-yo by
gathering a circle of calico with
a simple running stitch.

Personalize it!
Cut out a letter
from a doubled piece of felt and stitch
them together with embroidery floss.

Red and white pipe
cleaners twisted together
can become a fun candy cane to keep!
Twist two candy canes together and
make a heart package topper.

Handcrafted gifts like this mini scarf are a great way to send along a hug to a friend or loved one! Whether you make one for someone special or a bunch to drop off at a local nursing home, shelter or school, the warmth of your thoughtfulness will last all winter long.

Easy Neck Cozy

Ever tossed a wool sweater in the wash by mistake? Turn a felted sweater into two or three thoughtful gifts!

felted sweater
scissors

vintage buttons
needle & thread

If sweater is not a solid color, consider the pattern of the sweater and decide how it can best be used for this project. Once you have a suitable area identified, you're ready to cut your base. For kids, cut a rectangle measuring 4" wide and 18" to 20" long or, for adults, cut out a piece 6" wide and 30" to 32" long. Sew buttons onto one end and using the illustration on the next page as a guide, cut buttonholes to match up ends.

Don't have a felted sweater hanging around?
Shop thrift or second-hand stores for brightly colored
wool sweaters, toss in a hot water wash and dry on high...
they'll come out ready to use. It couldn't be easier!

*This nifty gift is easy to whip up in a jiffy
and smells good enough to eat!*

Vanilla-Brown Sugar Scrub

*Made from grocery-store ingredients, this scrub will leave skin smooth and
glowing…add a drizzle of honey for extra moisturizing!*

1 c. brown sugar, packed
1/2 c. sweet almond oil

2 vitamin E capsules
1/2 t. vanilla extract

Combine brown sugar and almond oil in a mixing bowl. Pierce capsules
with a knife or cut in half with kitchen scissors. Empty oil into sugar
mixture and discard capsules. Add vanilla and stir well to combine. Store
in an airtight container. Makes about one cup.

Pour into a jar with a rubber seal, add the label on the next page
and surprise someone who could use a little pampering.

Vanilla-Brown Sugar Scrub

Make a color copy of this label, cut out and glue to your jar before giving...add a little ribbon and it makes a great gift tag too!

Priscilla has been a long-time family friend and lives nearby. She's as active as someone half her age and was an avid skier until her mid-70s. Originally from Switzerland, she doesn't have family nearby but has enjoyed watching my children grow from toddlers to teens.

Throughout the years, she's become like a treasured aunt to our children. One Christmas, when my daughter Sydney was about five, she asked why Priscilla didn't celebrate with her family like we did. I explained that they lived far away and reminded her of Priscilla's vivid stories about growing up in Switzerland.

When we were doing our holiday shopping, Sydney was determined to find something that would remind Priscilla of home. When she happened upon a sparkly snow globe with a tiny skier inside, we both knew that it was perfect for our friend.

Just last Christmas, Priscilla recalled the year long ago when Sydney proudly carried her special gift up the steps to her door and how much she treasures her thoughtfulness.

~Jo Ann

Kind words

can be short and easy to speak,
but their echoes are truly endless.

~ *Mother Teresa*

Kids of all ages love to help others, given an opportunity and a little encouragement. Small kindnesses (or even big ones from little hands) can mean as much to the giver as the recipient, so let them lend a hand.

Wondering how to get your favorite little people involved?

Start small...for very young children, kindness starts at home. Let them help with younger siblings, pets, even household activities. Being an active part of their family community instills a feeling of value...plus, it lets them get a taste of how good "thank you!" can feel!

On the next page, we've gathered our favorite starting points but the possibilities for getting kids involved are as limitless as you choose.

Just remember these two things...

♥ No matter what their age, keep it simple...giving back doesn't have to be a big time commitment for it to turn into a lifelong habit.

♥ Reward even the smallest kindnesses with encouragement and praise!

*Let the passions and interests of older kids
be your guide when finding ways for them
to help out in their community.*

♥ Do they love animals? Perhaps helping at a shelter
would be great...they're always looking for dog-walkers
and kitty-petters. You could also spend the day baking
treats for dogs and cats at the shelter.

♥ Are they lucky enough to have close relationships
with grandparents or great-grandparents?
Spending time at a nursing home with residents
who don't have family close-by or even helping
an elderly neighbor rake leaves or plant flowers
would be fun.

♥ Do they love being outdoors? Maybe not at Christmas,
but planning to help the parks department picking up
litter in the spring or planting bulbs in the fall may
appeal to them.

Regardless of where kids end up donating their time
(or allowances!), the important thing is that warm & fuzzy
feeling we all get when we help others, at the holidays
and all year 'round.

Spend a day in the kitchen mixing up these treats for the family pet or friendly dogs in the neighborhood...double the recipe and take a big batch over to the local animal shelter. What a great way to wish our four-legged friends a Merry Christmas too!

Doggone Peanut Butter Biscuits
They'll be enjoyed with barks of delight!

2 c. whole-wheat flour
1 T. baking powder
1 c. chunky peanut butter

1 c. milk
all-purpose flour
   for dusting

Combine whole-wheat flour and baking powder in a mixing bowl; set aside. In a separate bowl, stir together peanut butter and milk; add to dry ingredients and mix well. Knead dough on a lightly floured surface to combine completely. Roll to 1/4-inch thickness and cut out with a cookie cutter. Transfer to a greased baking sheet and bake at 350 degrees for 15 to 20 minutes, until golden. Cool on a wire rack and store in an airtight container. Makes 20 to 30 biscuits.

If your kids or grandkids are old enough to get an allowance, try this fun twist on giving back and learning to save!

Set up three jars labeled Save, Spend and Give. When they get their weekly allowance, you can split it amongst the jars or let them decide how much goes in each.

At the end of the month, decide where the Give dollars will go and make a special trip to drop off their donation. Follow their good deed by enjoying a splurge from the Spend fund!

The ideas that have lighted
my way have been

kindness,

beauty and truth.

~ Albert Einstein

Get the whole gang involved when you host a holiday

party with a purpose!

In lieu of exchanging gifts, everyone brings $10 or $20 and information about a group that they'd like to help.

While enjoying great food and merriment, everyone shares their information with the group and, at the end of the evening, take a vote and choose your favorite cause.

Collect all the donations to send to the charity of choice!

Index

Savory Recipes

Sweet Recipes

Index

Crafts

Special Sections